A Guide for Using

Julie of the Wolves

in the Classroom

**Based on the novel written by
Jean Craighead George**

This guide written by Philip Denny

Illustrated by Sue Fullam

Teacher Created Resources, Inc.
6421 Industry Way
Westminster, CA 92683
www.teachercreated.com
©*1997 Teacher Created Resources, Inc.*
Reprinted, 2004
Made in U.S.A.
ISBN 1-55734-418-3

Table of Contents

◆ Quiz
◆ Hands-On Project—*Signals*
◆ Cooperative Learning Activity—*Miming*
◆ Curriculum Connections—*Geography: Alaska*
◆ Into Your Life—*Reading Response Journals*

◆ Quiz
◆ Hands-On-Project—*The Dream*
◆ Cooperative Learning Activity—*Teach Me!*
◆ Curriculum Connections—*Art: Recreate a Scene*
◆ Into Your Life—*Map Making*

◆ Quiz
◆ Hands-On Project—*Pride in Your Culture*
◆ Cooperative Learning Activity—*Points of View*
◆ Curriculum Connections—*Language Arts: Find Out More*
◆ Into Your Life—*Civilization*

◆ Quiz
◆ Hands-On Project—*Be Prepared!*
◆ Cooperative Learning Activity—*Overnighter*
◆ Curriculum Connections—*Science: The Wolf*
◆ Into Your Life—*Memories*

◆ Quiz
◆ Hands-On Project—*Igloo Project*
◆ Cooperative Learning Activity—*Imagine That!*
◆ Curriculum Connections—*Astronomy: The Solar System*
◆ Into Your Life—*Environmental Alert*

After the Book *(Post-reading Activities)*

Introduction

A good book can touch our lives like a good friend. Within its pages are words and characters that can inspire us to achieve our highest ideals. We can turn to it for companionship, recreation, comfort, and guidance. It can also give us a cherished story to hold in our hearts forever.

In *Literature Units,* great care has been taken to select books that are sure to become good friends!

Teachers who use this unit will find the following features to supplement their own valuable ideas.

- Sample Lesson Plans

- Pre-reading Activities

- A Biographical Sketch and Picture of the Author

- A Book Summary

- Vocabulary Lists and Suggested Vocabulary Activities

- Chapters grouped for study with each section including:

  – *quizzes*
  – *hands-on projects*
  – *cooperative learning activities*
  – *cross-curriculum connections*
  – *extensions into the reader's own life*

- Post-reading Activities

- Book Report Ideas

- Research Ideas

- Culminating Activity

- Three Different Options for Unit Tests

- Bibliography

- Answer Key

We are confident this unit will be a valuable addition to your planning, and we hope your students will increase the circle of "friends" they have in books as you use our ideas!

Sample Lesson Plan

Lesson 1
- Introduce and complete some or all of the prereading activities found on page 5.
- Read "About the Author" with your students. (page 6)
- Introduce the vocabulary list for Section 1. (page 8) Ask students to define these words.

Lesson 2
- Read pages 5 through 37. As you read, place the vocabulary words in the context of the story and discuss their meanings.
- Play a vocabulary game. (page 9)
- Form systems of non-verbal communication. (page 11)
- Practice miming simple commands. (page 12)
- Make a map of Alaska. (page 13)
- Begin "Reading Response Journals." (page 14)
- Administer the Section 1 quiz. (page 10)
- Introduce the vocabulary list for Section 2. (page 8) Ask students to define these words.

Lesson 3
- Read pages 37-70. Place the vocabulary words in context and discuss their meanings.
- Play a vocabulary game. (page 9)
- Create a dream sequence for Miyax. (page 16)
- Teach a unique skill to your classmates. (page 17)
- Illustrate scenes from the story. (page 18)
- Make a map of how to get to local landmarks. (page 19)
- Administer Section 2 quiz. (page 15)
- Introduce the vocabulary list for Section 3. (page 8) Ask students to define these words.

Lesson 4
- Read pages 75-104. Place the vocabulary words in context and discuss their meanings.
- Play a vocabulary game. (page 9)
- Complete "Pride in Your Culture." (page 21)
- Make a list of Kapugen's values before and after his wife died. (page 22)
- Find out about the people of Alaska. (page 23)
- Investigate the effects of industrial advances in Alaska. (page 24)
- Administer Section 3 quiz. (page 20)
- Introduce the vocabulary list for Section 4. (page 8) Ask students to define these words.

Lesson 5
- Read pages 109-138. Place the vocabulary words in context and discuss their meanings.
- Play a vocabulary game. (page 9)
- Determine what provisions would be necessary in emergency situations. (page 26)
- Create an overnight survival kit using natural materials. (page 27)
- Research an animal from Alaska's wilds; present reports to class. (page 28)
- Recall incidents from life that seemed hopeless and their resolutions. (page 30)
- Administer Section 4 quiz. (page 25)
- Introduce the vocabulary list for Section 5. (page 8) Ask students to define these words.

Lesson 6
- Read pages 138-170. Place the vocabulary words in context and discuss their meanings.
- Play a vocabulary game. (page 9)
- Build an igloo. (page 32)
- Write a reunion scene of Miyax with her father. (page 33)
- Learn more about astronomy. (page 34)
- Write and deliver a speech about cleaning up the Alaskan environment. (page 35)
- Administer Section 5 quiz. (page 31)

Lesson 7
- Discuss any questions your students may have about the story. (page 35)
- Assign book report and research projects. (pages 37 and 38)
- Begin work on a culminating activity. (pages 39, 40, and 41) Lesson 8
- Administer Unit Test: 1, 2, and/or 3. (pages 42, 43, and 44)
- Discuss the test answers and possibilities.
- Discuss the students' enjoyment of the book.
- Provide a list of related reading for your students. (page 45)

Before the Book

Before you begin reading *Julie of the Wolves* with your students, do some pre-reading activities to stimulate interest and enhance comprehension. Here are some activities that might work well in your class.

1. Predict what the story might be about just by hearing the title.

2. Predict what the story might be about just by looking at the cover illustration.

3. Discuss other books by Jean Craighead George that students may have heard or read about.

4. Answer these questions:

   • Would you like to read...

      – stories of adventure?
      – stories involving nature?
      – stories involving children overcoming hardships?
      – stories about environments different from your own?
      – stories of children having to make difficult decisions?

   • Would you ever . . .

      – be able to walk 400 miles through the wilderness alone?
      – be able to make friends with wild animals?
      – learn to use nature's resources for months at a time to survive?
      – learn to find adequate food to survive a winter in the wilderness?

5. Have you ever learned to communicate with an animal?

   Describe the animal and the types of communication you established in detail.

6. Work in a group to make a story outline of a 400-mile trip through Alaska.

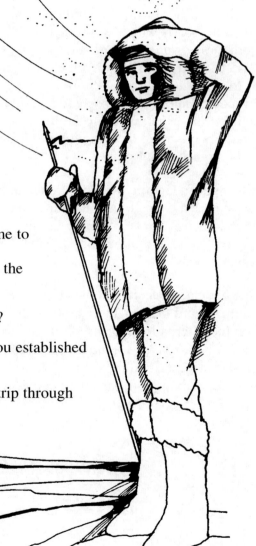

About the Author

Jean Craighead George was born July 12, 1919, in the nation's capital, Washington D.C., to Frank and Carolyn Craighead. She attended Pennsylvania State University where she received her B.A. degree in 1941. She continued her studies at Louisiana State University and the University of Michigan. Her marriage to John George took place in 1944, and they have three children. Today she lives in Chappaqua, New York.

She began her career right out of college where she worked for International News Service as a reporter in the town of her birth, Washington, D.C. Here she polished her skills which served her as she worked on both the *Washington Post* and the *Times-Herald*. In 1945 she moved to New York City, working as an artist for *Pageant* and as a reporter-artist for "Newspaper Enterprise Association." After leaving these jobs, she began working full time as a writer. Her early books were created with her husband, and then she branched out on her own.

Jean Craighead George's novels are about nature. Although there is diversity in her novels, the books often have themes in common. Her characters such as Miyax in *Julie of the Wolves*, study nature and try to unlock its secrets. Along with heralding the sanctity and beauty of nature, she writes of man's impact on nature and of ecology themes. All of these themes are evident in *Julie of the Wolves* as in her other novels.

During her career, Jean Craighead George has been given many awards and honors. She received the Aurianne Award of the American Library Association for *Dipper of Copper Creek*, 1958. In 1969 she was on the International Hans Christian Anderson Award honor list and a John Newbery Medal runner-up for *My Side of the Mountain*. After being voted Pennsylvania State College "Woman of the Year" in 1969, she was awarded the "Book World First Prize" in 1971 for *Once Upon a Stone*. These are just a few of the many honors bestowed upon this productive author.

6

Julie of the Wolves

by Jean Craighead George
(Harper and Row, 1972)
(Also available in Canada, U.K and Australia from Harper Collins)

Miyax is an Eskimo girl living in Alaska. While Miyax is still young, her mother dies, and she lives alone with her father at a seal camp. Miyax learns of the old ways. She is happy living in the traditional Eskimo manner, learning of her people's traditions and customs.

However, the law expects her to attend school. Her life changes dramatically when she is forced to leave the seal camp to live with her aunt and return to civilization. She leaves and attends the school where she experiences prejudice for the first time. She begins to feel ashamed of her people's backward ways.

By chance, she gets a pen pal named Amy. It is Amy who calls her Julie, and opens up a new world for her. Miyax dreams of leaving Alaska and going to San Francisco where a special pink room overlooking the bay is waiting for her. As life becomes increasingly unbearable with her demanding aunt, she yearns for this magical city with its Golden Gate, television sets, and fancy Opera Houses.

Suddenly her life again changes. At 13 years of age she flies to Barrow, Alaska, for a marriage arranged by her father. Her life here is just as bad. Her father-in-law is a drunk and constantly beats his wife. Then, the unexpected happens—her husband, Daniel, assaults her. This is the catalyst that forces her to act.

Miyax sets out for San Francisco. She soon finds herself alone, lost in the vast tundra without a compass or the North Star to guide her, as it is summer and the sun does not set. In fact, it will not set for over a month. She also is out of food.

The rest of the story is of her courage, determination and self-discovery. While studying a pack of wolves and communicating with them, her pride in her people's wisdom and tradition is restored. She becomes accepted as a member of the wolves' den. She learns of progress. She comes to question what "civilization" really means to her people. She sees how "civilization" has taken her people's dignity away and replaced it with pollution and alcohol. She sees it as a monster. At its conclusion this story answers as many questions as it leaves to be answered. The reader is left to believe that Miyax will search for the answers.

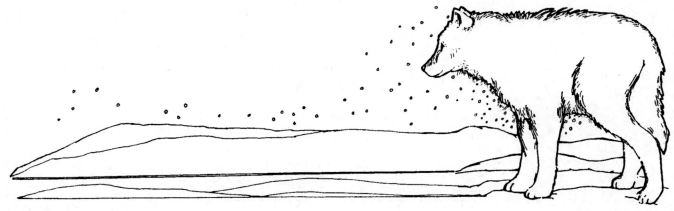

Vocabulary List

On this page are vocabulary lists which correspond to each sectional grouping of chapters. Vocabulary activity ideas can be found on page 9 of this book.

Section 1
Pages 5-37

parka	Arctic	vast	harpoon	mimicking
cosmos	caribou	kayak	discern	triggered
signal	pack	ignored	glistened	undulating
environment	rigorous	lichens	lemmings	acutely

Section 2
Pages 37-70

drastically	shank	den	pondered	harmonized
white-outs	tundra	hostile	nomadic	diligently
buntings	sedge	plummeting	laboriously	migrated
acute	quell	incorrigible	immobile	menacingly

Section 3
Pages 75-104

deserted	grieving	reindeer	shaman	anxiety
blizzard	tusks	velveteen	ridiculous	reluctant
derisively	domestic	corporation	enchanted	vibrant
prosperous	moosehide	miraculous	escorted	pinnacles

Section 4
Pages 109-138

eerie	speckled	brandishing	humbly	concave
abeyance	antler	gingerly	sinew	immense
niche	stout	browsed	compass	improvised
bellowing	cumbersome	guidepost	abruptly	harassing

Section 5
Pages 138-170

scurrying	slump	sustain	pensions	veered
frigid	grandeur	romping	constricted	artifacts
yearling	engulfed	massive	emeralds	totem
resonant	enveloped	distressed	tanned	snares

Vocabulary Activity Ideas

You can help your students learn and retain the vocabulary in *Julie of the Wolves* by providing them with interesting vocabulary activities. Here are a few ideas to try.

❏ People of all ages like to make and solve puzzles. Ask your students to make their own **Crossword Puzzles** or **Wordsearch Puzzles** using the vocabulary words from the story.

❏ Challenge your students to a **Vocabulary Bee!** This is similar to a spelling bee, but in addition to spelling each word correctly, the game participants must correctly define the words as well.

❏ Play **Vocabulary Concentration**. The goal of this game is to match vocabulary words with their definitions. Divide the class into groups of 2-5 students. Have students make two sets of cards the same size and color. On one set have them write the vocabulary words. On the second set have them write the definitions. All cards are mixed together and placed face down on a table. A player picks two cards. If the pair matches the word with its definition, the player keeps the cards and takes another turn. If the cards do not match, they are returned to their places face down on the table, and another player takes a turn. Players must concentrate to remember the locations of the words and their definitions. The game continues until all matches have been made. This is an ideal activity for free exploration time.

❏ Have your students practice their writing skills by creating sentences and paragraphs in which multiple vocabulary words are used correctly. Ask them to share their **Compact Vocabulary** sentences and paragraphs with the class.

❏ Challenge your students to use a specific vocabulary word from the story at least **10 Times In One Day**. They must keep a record of when, how, and why the word was used!

❏ As a group activity, have students work together to create an **Illustrated Dictionary** of the vocabulary words.

❏ Play **20 Clues** with the entire class. In this game, one student selects a vocabulary word and gives clues about this word, one by one, until someone in the class can guess the word.

❏ Play **Vocabulary Charades**. In this game, vocabulary words are acted out.

You probably have many more ideas to add to this list. Try them! See if experiencing vocabulary on a personal level increases your students' vocabulary interest and retention.

Quiz

1. On the back of this paper, write a one-paragraph summary of the major events in this section. Then complete the rest of the questions on this page.

2. Why is Miyax so interested in the wolves?

   _____

   _____

3. By studying these wolves what does Miyax hope to learn?

   _____

   _____

4. What does Miyax want to communicate to these wolves?

   _____

   _____

5. Why does Miyax name the black pup Kapugen?

   _____

   _____

6. Why is Miyax alone in the Arctic tundra?

   _____

   _____

7. How is the tundra different from Miyax's home on Nunivak Island where she never could get lost?

   _____

   _____

8. Where does Miyax hope to walk for help?

   _____

   _____

9. Why does Miyax have an interest in the ship called *The North Star*?

   _____

   _____

10. Describe the shelter that Miyax makes for herself.

    _____

    _____

Signals

Several times we see Miyax studying the wolves. She is trying to read them for clues as to how the wolves communicate with each other. She thinks that if she can imitate these signals, she will be able to talk with them as her father once had done. Her father disappeared before telling her how this was accomplished.

  A. What did Amaroq command her to do when he first communicated with her?

      _____

      _____

  B. What signals did he give her to tell her that she had better do this?

      _____

      _____

Miyax finally concluded that when Amaroq clamps or bites the top of the other wolves' noses, he is asserting himself as leader. To show respect or obedience, the wolves in his pack bit Amaroq's lower jaw or simply rolled on their backs in a signal of submission.

By studying the puppies and adults, Miyax confirms her new language—wolf talk. Then, after she practices with Kapu and Sister, she finally is able to make friends with Amaroq.

To start your class thinking about nonverbal communication, ask a student to "tell" you, without using any words and from a distance, to move to a specific place in the room. After several students have tried, introduce the following activity.

Divide the class into groups of 8 to 20, the size of a wolf pack. Have them decide who will be the leader. Within the group, they are to create a system of communication that does not use any words. Everyone in the group must understand the system and be able to use it. The system should be able to accomplish one or more of the following tasks:

    1. direct someone to move to a specific place in the classroom
    2. direct someone to place a series of objects in a specific order
    3. direct someone to draw several geometric shapes in a specific arrangement

If task 2 or 3 are chosen, show students ahead of time the objects and geometric shapes about which they will be communicating.

Prepare several cards for each task. For Task 1, simply list specific room locations; e.g., closet door, big window, Suki's desk, northwest corner. For Task 2 make drawings (or a list) of the five or more selected objects in a different order on each card. For Task 3 draw the selected geometric shapes in a different arrangement on each card.

When the groups are ready with their signal system, have a group member choose a card at random and direct a groupmate. After everyone has had a turn, compare the signal systems developed by each group. Were there any similarities?

Miming

We are all excellent observers. Whether on a trip, going to a concert, or simply going shopping at the mall, we all are constantly reading people and situations as they occur. We are able to use previous personal experiences learned from our family and friends as guidelines for observations.

Working with a partner, first describe these typical commands and what they indicate. In the boxes below, write or draw how each might be communicated. When you are finished think of some simple commands such as "No!," "Wait," "Good bye," and "You're Safe," that you and your partner might want to communicate to each other. Practice sharing them with the class. Have classmates guess what they might be.

Stop!	**Be quiet.**
Come here.	**Look.**
Speak up.	**I don't know.**

Geography: Alaska

For this assignment you must consult your research books. You are being asked to set the scene and setting for this survival part of the story.

Include all the major cities, rivers, mountain ranges, and bodies of water that surround this state. Make sure you label each of these geological and topographical formations. You should include a compass and a color code for your elevations. Put an X where Julie is located and draw a dotted line where she came from and where she has to go to catch the ship.

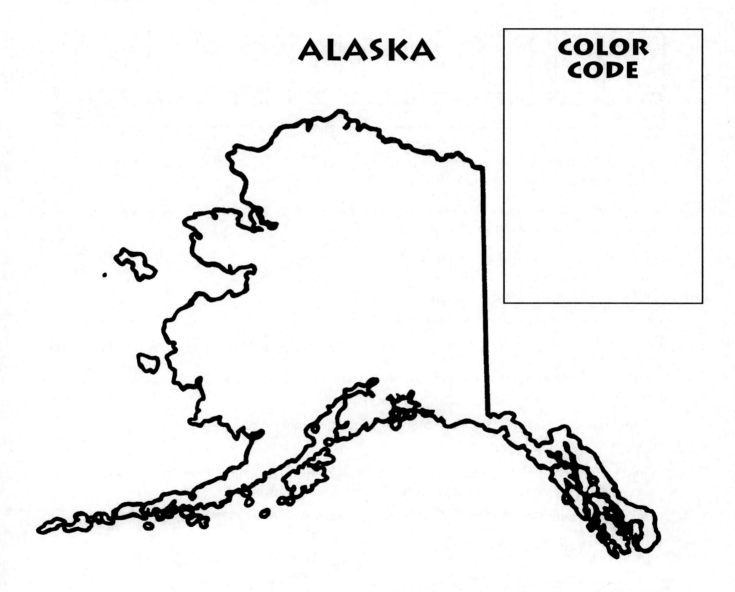

Reading Response Journals

One great way to ensure that the reading of *Julie of the Wolves* touches each student in a personal way is to include the use of Reading Response Journals in your plans. In these journals, students can be encouraged to respond to the story in a number of ways. Here are a few ideas.

• Ask students to create a journal for *Julie of the Wolves*. Initially, have them assemble lined and unlined, three-holed paper in a brad-fastened "report cover", with a blank page for the journal's cover. As they read the story, they may draw a design on the cover that helps tell the story for them.

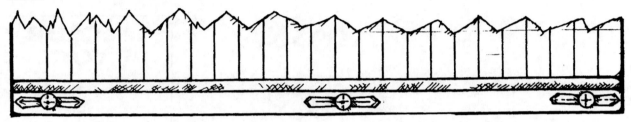

• Tell them that the purpose of the journal is to record their thoughts, ideas, observations, and questions as they read *Julie of the Wolves*.

• Provide students with, or ask them to suggest, topics from the story that would stimulate writing. Here are a few examples from the pages in Section 1.

> What did Daniel do that drove Julie into the wilderness?
> Was she really married at age 13?
> Why did she leave Barrow without a compass?
> If you were in her place alone with no food, how would you feel?

• After reading each section, students can write one or more new things they learned in the chapter.

• Ask students to draw their responses to certain events or characters in the story, using the blank pages in their journals.

• Tell students that they may use their journals to record "diary type" responses that they want to enter.

• Encourage students to bring their journal ideas to life! Ideas generated from their journal writing can be used to create plays, debates, stories, songs, and art displays.

Allow students time to write in their journals daily.

See the answer key for ideas for the evaluation of your students' Reading Response Journals.

Quiz

1. On the back of this paper, write a one-paragraph summary of the major events that happen in this section. Then complete the rest of the questions on this page.

2. Which of the caribou do the wolves seem to single out for their kill?

   _____

   _____

3. Why do the wolves choose this type over the others?

   _____

   _____

4. Why does Miyax shudder in fear when she notices that the wolves had open-ended tunnels for their den?

   _____

   _____

5. What does Miyax remember that her father told her which calms her down and enables her to find food?

   _____

   _____

6. What surprising thing does Amaroq do after he slashed the mitten to pieces?

   _____

   _____

7. How does the heavy fog bring Miyax a way to make a type of compass?

   _____

   _____

8. What feelings does Miyax have for Amaroq?

   _____

   _____

9. Where does Miyax store all her smoked caribou?

   _____

   _____

10. Why is Amy's letter so important to Miyax?

    _____

    _____

The Dream

This last section ended with Miyax falling asleep with Amy's letter tucked under her cheek. This letter was valuable to her as it represented her escape from the Eskimo way of life, from the dreary trash heap of Barrow and most importantly from her husband, Daniel. In striking contrast to her sorrowful life is the dazzling world of San Francisco. Her new pink room on a hill in San Francisco with a view of the Golden Gate Bridge and the bay all waited for her. She already had a friend, Amy who was ready to take her to places she could only dream about.

You are the dream-maker. After the part which says, "That night she slept with the letter under her cheek," write about Miyax's dream of San Francisco. Using what you know from the story and of how Miyax lived previously, describe her night-time visions of her life in San Francisco. Remember that it is this dream that gives her the strength to survive being lost and makes her so determined to reach her new life. Use the thought bubble to write the dream.

Teach Me!

In this section we see how Miyax has been able to learn many things from the wolves. She also learns from Amy and from her father as well as from others. We learn by observing and by doing. As a class, brainstorm and think of things that your class knows how to do. Try to think of things that can be learned in a short period of time. The following is a partial list to get you started:

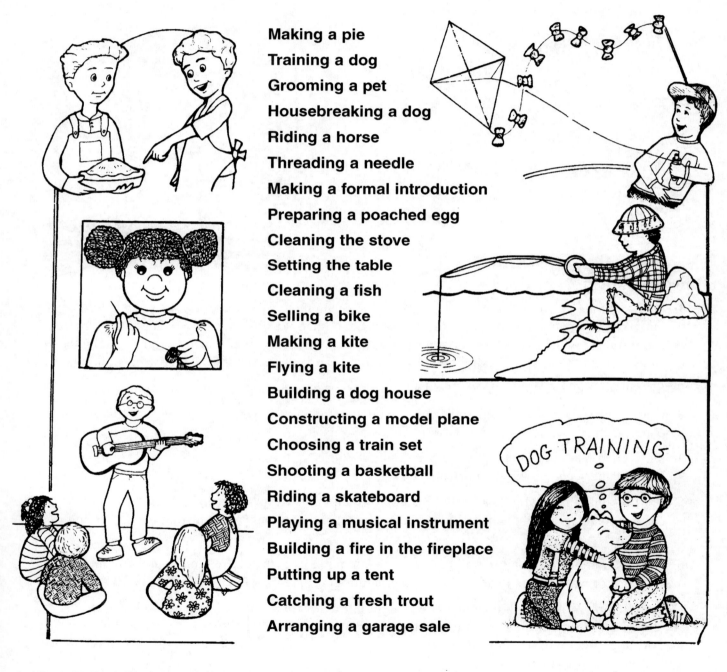

Making a pie

Training a dog

Grooming a pet

Housebreaking a dog

Riding a horse

Threading a needle

Making a formal introduction

Preparing a poached egg

Cleaning the stove

Setting the table

Cleaning a fish

Selling a bike

Making a kite

Flying a kite

Building a dog house

Constructing a model plane

Choosing a train set

Shooting a basketball

Riding a skateboard

Playing a musical instrument

Building a fire in the fireplace

Putting up a tent

Catching a fresh trout

Arranging a garage sale

After you have brainstormed, team up with a classmate. Try to teach your partner a skill that you know. Then have your partner teach you a new skill. Together decide which skill you would like to perfect and share it with the class. Bring appropriate samples of your topic to share with the class.

Art: Recreate a Scene

Near the end of this section, Miyax realized that autumn was upon her. The birds were heading south, and the sun was halfway below the horizon. The sky turned navy blue, the clouds turned bright yellow, and twilight was upon the land. On the horizon as well she earlier noticed hundreds of black fingers—the antlers of the caribou silhouetted against the skyline.

To recreate the scene, follow the directions below.

You will need the following supplies:

- crayons

- water colors

- white construction paper

- paint brushes (thin, medium and broad)

- white paper

- pencils

Directions:

1. On a separate piece of white paper, organize the scene that you are about to recreate. If you are not going to include anything but the horizon scene, then you will probably want to have more room for the scene above the horizon. If you plan to include animals such as moose, deer, the snowy owl, etc. in your tundra, then you should arrange the two scenes equally, half for each.

2. Sketch out the scene described above adding any special touches you think appropriate.

3. Once your sketch meets your satisfaction, you are ready to transfer it to the white construction paper, using crayons and paints to dramatize the effects.

4. On your construction paper, use crayon to draw your sun, birds, and clouds. Use bright colors here for the scene above the horizon.

5. For the tundra, use white and light blue crayons, and draw tufts of green and brown where the earth is visible. Here is where you will also draw in any animals as seen from Miyax's point of view.

6. Once you are finished with your crayon drawing, paint over the entire picture and crayon colors with bright watercolors to add depth to the painting.

   For example, if your sun is orange, you might put bold streaks of yellow across it. The white clouds can have smears of purple, yellow, or orange on the underside of them. When the paint dries the effect will be startling, since the water colors will not "stick" evenly on the crayon base but will on the paper.

7. For the final touch, cut a frame for your picture out of construction paper that matches one of your colors.

Map Making

Being lost is not something anyone would like to experience. Julie is truly in the middle of nowhere with winter coming on quickly. Anyone can get lost, but it might not be so bad if it were in your own town or city. Usually you could just ask a neighbor, storekeeper, or police officer where you are and how to get to where you want to go.

Working with a partner make a map. Your map should show how you get from your house to any wellknown location in your town, city, or state. It should include important, well-known buildings or geographical formations such as rivers, mountains, oceans. Include a directional compass, a symbol key, and a distance scale. Use the space below to create your map. After completing the map, write directions in clear, easy-to-understand language.

Key

Directions:

Quiz

1. On the back of this paper, write a one-paragraph summary of the major events that happen in this section. Then complete the rest of the questions on this page.

2. How old was Miyax when her mother died?

   _____

   _____

3. How did this death take its toll on her father, Kapugen?

   _____

   _____

4. Why do the hunters always return the inflated seal bladders to the sea?

   _____

   _____

5. When is it that Miyax learns that if you talk to a wolf, the wolf will love you?

   _____

   _____

6. Why does Miyax get upset when her father called her "Julie?"

   _____

   _____

7. Why does Miyax prefer the winters to the summers?

   _____

   _____

8. What bad news does Martha bring that changes Miyax's life?

   _____

   _____

9. Describe how Miyax's life changes when she goes to live with her aunt in Mekoryuk.

   _____

   _____

10. What makes Miyax think that she can make the trip across Alaska on foot?

   _____

   _____

Pride in Your Culture

In this section of the book the plot becomes more complicated. Miyax, who had always taken pride in being an Eskimo, becomes confused as to her identity. She once stamped her foot when her father called her Julie in the manner of the gussaks. These were Eskimos who were educated in English and adopted the American ways over their own. She was proud of her father and of being an Eskimo.

As we read, however, when she is taken away and sent to an English speaking school, she learns to be embarrassed with her "old-fashioned" ways. The other students laugh at her ignorance. Somehow her world as she once knew it begins slipping away. She ends up throwing her once-prized possession away. Then, with her new pen pal in San Francisco painting a whole new world, she becomes dissatisfied with her old life and is determined to go live the exciting life in the modern world.

There are many people in America, and we come from a variety of interesting places around the world. Each location has its own customs and traditions, feast days and celebrations to be proud of and to be preserved. An example for Miyax would be the simple celebration of the Bladder Feast and the warmth it meant for her people and of life in general.

What special customs and celebrations are there among your own friends and neighbors? Interview them to find out. Use the categories below to compile information. Find at least three individuals to survey. When you have finished gathering information share what you have learned.

Survey	Survey	Survey
Person's name:	Person's name:	Person's name:
Original Homeland:	Original Homeland:	Original Homeland:
Special Celebrations:	Special Celebrations:	Special Celebrations:
Unique Customs:	Unique Customs:	Unique Customs:
Traditional Customs:	Traditional Customs:	Traditional Customs:

Points of View

In the flashback sequence we see that Miyax becomes confused about her life and her values. While a young child, she lived with her father at the seal camp. She treasured these times. She tells of the various things she remembered of her early life.

She tells of going into her father's simple little house, of how it was "golden-brown" with neat walrus tusks and "harpoons, and man's knives" decorating the walls. She went on seal hunts with her father and participated in the Eskimo celebrations with pride. All these things conflicted with her new lifestyle. Martha indirectly sends the message that her early life was nothing. She tells Miyax that her father "walked away to a seal camp, and he never did anything good after that."

What a blow it must have been to Miyax when Martha mocked her great memories as valueless. Martha was talking about Miyax's fondest memories! Then, when her *i'noGo tied* was laughed at by the students of the English school, she was so confused and ashamed she threw it away.

If you are from a certain culture and have a particular way of thinking, that does not mean that other cultures and ways are of no consequence. They are respected by the members who value what their heritage believes. Obviously, Miyax's father would disagree that the old life was "nothing" as earlier suggested.

With your partner write down various things which were important to Kapugen. These should be things that he either said were important or that he took great pride in. Include the animals and other aspects of nature that he thought special. While doing this assignment remember the kind of life he had before and the material possessions that he left behind to recapture his older value system. After you have the ideas and things that he valued written down, create another list of values and things that he would find unimportant in life. Compare these and report to the class.

Important	**Unimportant**
_____	_____
_____	_____
_____	_____
_____	_____
_____	_____
_____	_____
_____	_____
_____	_____

Language Arts: Find Out More

The Eskimos are the natives of the sea coasts in the Arctic regions of Alaska and Eastern Siberia. They originally were great hunters. Europeans gave them their name Eskimo, which means "eaters of raw meat." They, however, call themselves the Inuit, which means "real people."

Eskimos have traditionally lived as hunters on the coastal regions, hunting seals, walrus, and whales. Some hunters follow the caribou, as did the wolves, inland during the warmer summer months. Although groups of Inuits live all along a coastline 8,000 miles long, it is interesting that their religion, social activities, and economics are essentially identical to one another.

For the following activities you and your partner will need to go to the library or some other place which will give you access to reference books on Alaska.

Research and supply the information for the following.

Eskimo Economy

1. What are the natural resources?

2. What are their main sources of income?

3. Are there any new income opportunities in their future?

4. Do the economic opportunities conflict with their traditional way of life? (Explain how.)

Eskimo Religion

1. Describe their religious beliefs.

2. How are their religious leaders chosen?

3. Describe any special ceremonies they might perform.

Eskimo Housing

1. Describe what a typical village is like.

2. While hunting in the Arctic, the Inuit often made a temporary shelter called an igloo. Briefly describe this ancient form of shelter.

    A. Its history

    B. How it is built

    C. How it becomes "sealed" and what they used for windows

Civilization

Miyax's confusion must have seemed even greater after she took her trip to Barrow, Alaska. She was going to an outpost which was inhabited by many Americans. These were Amy's people, people who were civilized and knew only the good life. She often thought of Amy, the big neat house with the arched doorway, Persian rugs on the floor and sunny rooms with windows that looked out onto the bay.

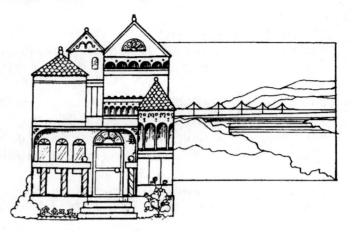

Imagine her dismay, then, when she arrived in Barrow only to see the cluttered streets. Rags and trash were everywhere. The little houses were huddled up against the broken ice fields like a "cluster of lonely birds." And these were surrounded by old "boats, oil drums, tires, buckets and broken cars."

Since many tourists come, there is a thriving community of Eskimos who have jobs and make money. But this money does not always bring happiness. Her new father-in-law, for one, periodically is gone for nights at a time on drunken binges. Sometimes he ends up in jail, and other times he returns home full of "evil" to beat his wife. Even here in remote Alaska, civilization brings with it a high price—misery.

Brainstorm the negative impact civilization and its "improvements" have unwittingly brought to today's society. While there are benefits there are also negative side effects that can take place. Write your ideas here. Share your thoughts with the class.

_____

_____

_____

_____

_____

_____

Use the information gathered through the brainstorming activity to create a poster that will show some industrialized improvement from which we benefit and the negative side effects it brings.

Quiz

1. On the back of this paper, write a one-paragraph summary of the major events in this section.

2. Although Miyax is ready to go with the wolves in the morning, what does she find when she arrives at the wolves' den?

   _____

   _____

3. What does Miyax tell the owl when it looks at her curiously?

   _____

   _____

4. When Miyax returns to her camp after going to Amaroq's den, what new obstacle does she find for herself?

   _____

   _____

5. Although Miyax endures a great deal, what is her mood after consulting her compass and heading off toward Point Hope?

   _____

   _____

6. After Miyax discovers that the cowardly Jello has stolen her provisions and food, what does the wolf pack do to right this wrong?

   _____

   _____

7. After she recovers her pack and its possessions, what does she discover within herself that made reaching Point Hope less important?

   _____

   _____

8. Why does Miyax have trouble concentrating on the visions or dreams of San Francisco?

   _____

   _____

9. What does Kapu bring her that reinforces her feeling that she is becoming one with nature?

   _____

   _____

10. Why does the oil drum, "the signpost of American civilization," bring confusion instead of happiness to Miyax?

    _____

    _____

Be Prepared!

After the wolves left their den to do their winter hunting, Miyax was in good humor and quite prepared to travel up to Point Hope without the wolves' help. She had everything she needed in her pack. Some of the most important things were her needles, matches, and a man's knife.

Describe why she needed the following items.

1. needles _____

_____

2. matches _____

_____

3. man's knife_____

_____

4. bones _____

_____

5. sinew _____

_____

We often read about hikers in the mountains who are "caught off guard" by a summer storm or a blizzard which cuts them off from their home base.

One should always be prepared for an emergency situation. Below are three areas in which it is important to be prepared. Read each situation and follow the directions. Begin by numbering a paper 1 through 15.

Auto

On a piece of paper write five of the most important things which should be in your car at all times in case of an emergency. Next to each item, tell how it would be of use to you.

Backpacking

Add to this list the five mandatory items which you would include in your backpack if you were to go on an overnight hiking expedition in the mountains. Next to each item, tell how it would be of use to you.

Marine

The next five "musts" for your safety involve boating readiness. Add to your list five items which you feel are mandatory if you are going out to sea for a few days. Next to each tell how it would be of use to you.

Overnighter

After Jello stole Miyax's pack which held everything necessary for her to survive, she fully appreciated being an Eskimo and being able to "adjust to nature." She began to feel that the people at the old seal camp had not been as old-fashioned as she had been led to believe. They were, in fact, very wise. She was proud to be an Eskimo once more, for Eskimos were like scientists, too. After all, they used the plants, animals, and temperature to change the harsh Arctic into a home.

We see an example of this when Miyax constructs her tent. She wraps reeds together, puts them into freezing water, and lets them freeze. When she pulls them out, they miraculously become her strong tent poles so she can be protected from the winter snows and winds which are sure to batter her before her journey is over.

In this activity you are going to demonstrate that you, too, are able to survive in a natural environment.

With one or two partners, you are going to have one week to prepare for a two-night trip in the mountains. Just as Miyax has fashioned her survival items and materials, you will have to do the same. Your team will have a week to present to the class your creation, using things found in nature (where possible) for the following:

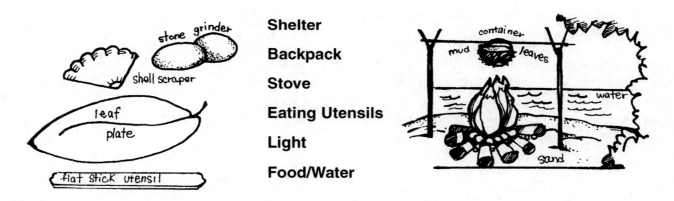

Shelter

Backpack

Stove

Eating Utensils

Light

Food/Water

In your presentation you will show your class how your shelter works. You will demonstrate how you will manage at night with a light source, what you will eat, and how you will prepare it. A recipe would be a nice touch, too. You will also have to show your homemade eating utensils and some sort of way to cook your evening feast. You cannot bring fast foods. You must be able to prepare something on a heat source.

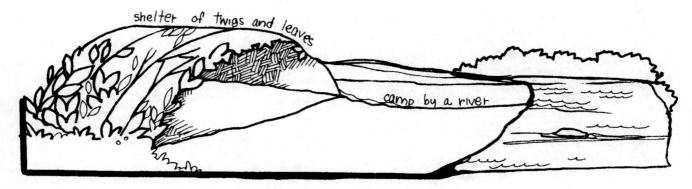

Science: The Wolf

Alaska, the largest game reserve in the United States, is the main habitat of the wolf. The gray wolf is a large animal and a member of the canine family. The male wolf has a length which reaches six and one half feet (195 cm). Its weight is about one hundred and twenty pounds (54 kg). An animal this big needs a large range of territory in which to operate and hunt. In fact, it has the second largest range of a terrestrial animal; only humans are greater.

Due to the extreme cold in Alaska and the Arctic, its fur becomes long and thick in the winter. It also changes from its gray summer color and reflects its winter surroundings by turning pure white to match its northern habitat. The gray wolf is sometimes referred to in literature as the "Arctic wolf" or "white wolf."

For defense and hunting the wolf is equipped with a strong jaw and four long fangs. These are up to two inches (5 cm) long and are used for killing, wounding, or pulling down its prey. It also has sharp side teeth which are used for tearing through muscle. Its back teeth are used to grind up and crush its victim's bones for swallowing. With its large stomach, it can eat twenty pounds (9 kg) of food at a time. This enables it to go for about two weeks between meals if it needs to do so.

The wolf's main prey is caribou, deer, elk, and moose. The size of the game it hunts determines the size of the individual wolf pack. If their main prey is moose, for instance, the usual size of the pack will be from 15-20 wolves. A smaller animal like a deer or caribou would be pursued by a pack of from 6-14 wolves.

The wolves provide a necessary function as they kill old or sick animals. This is a service as it strengthens the herd of its victim by providing more food for that herd, and it eliminates the sick members from the herd. This way there is enough food for the strong members, and disease is not transmitted throughout the herd, jeopardizing their existence.

Arctic or Alaskan Animal Report

In *Julie of the Wolves*, wolves play an important part in the story. Read the information on page 28 to find out more about wolves. There are many more animals found in the wilds of Alaska and the Arctic region. A partial list includes polar bears, the brown bear, moose, caribou, deer, Arctic foxes, reindeer, and elk. With your partner, consult an encyclopedia, a book about a specific animal, magazine articles, or other resource books and research an Alaskan or Arctic animal of your choice. Use the form below to help you organize your material.

Animal Report

Type of animal: _____

Size:_____

Height: _____

Length:_____

Weight _____

Describe its habitat and range. _____

_____

_____

Describe its enemies. _____

_____

_____

Describe any characteristics of its defense. _____

_____

_____

Describe its most interesting feature. _____

_____

_____

Resources used: _____

_____

Draw a picture of the animal in its natural environment. Attach it to your report.

Memories

In this section there have been many memorable scenes. One was the emotional experience suffered by Miyax when she discovered that Jello had trampled her shelter and eaten the food which she needed to survive her trek to Point Hope. She felt "needles of fear" moving up her spine and into her arms when she realized the significance of the loss. She sums up her feeling when she states in anguished tones,

"My food! My life! I'm dead!"

As we read on, we see that she does survive this incident only to have yet another experience try her indomitable spirit. Jello continues to be her plague as he returns yet again. This time he takes her pack containing her boots, knife, and items necessary to live in this harsh environment. She realizes that she can go nowhere without boots. She could not even fashion some new ones because her needles and ulo, "the tools of survival," were all in the pack. She just lay down and wondered how long it would take to die.

For each of these situations there were corresponding high points to counterbalance these low points.

Activity 1: In the space below, tell what happened in each of the two situations above that solved her life and death problems.

A. _____

_____

B. _____

_____

Activity 2: For this activity you must recall incidents from your own life that made you feel desperate, alone, or without hope. Using the space below explain what led up to the situation and then what happened to make you feel so "down." (A) After doing this, tell how the problem resolved itself. (B) If it did not get solved, relate how you were able to work through it.

A. _____

_____

_____

_____

B. _____

_____

_____

_____

Quiz

1. On the back of this paper, write a one-paragraph summary of the major events in this last section. Then complete the rest of the questions on this page.

2. What is the airplane doing that upsets Miyax?

   _____

   _____

3. Why does Miyax run to hide under the barrel?

   _____

   _____

4. How do the advances of "civilization" hurt Amaroq?

   _____

   _____

5. In her grief for Amaroq, why does Miyax speak only in Eskimo?

   _____

   _____

6. How does Miyax reduce the grief and keep Amaroq's spirit with her forever?

   _____

   _____

7. Why is it important for the wolf pack to have Kapu return?

   _____

   _____

8. What does the sighting of the Brooks Range mean to Miyax?

   _____

   _____

9. Who is it that helps give the town of Kangik back its pride and makes it independent and prosperous?

   _____

   _____

10. What is the significance when Miyax sings to Amaroq in English at the end of the story?

    _____

    _____

Igloo Project

As Julie walked closer and closer to her destination, her confusion became replaced by determination. She became more determined to avoid the trappings of civilization and decided to embrace the old ways of the traditional Eskimo. She finally sets up a permanent house so that she can think her future over carefully. Using her knife to cut out ice blocks of snow, she builds an igloo.

An igloo is the Eskimo name for a shelter. Traditional Eskimo shelters were made of snow, sod, or stone. The best-known igloo was the winter snowhouse of the Eskimo. In this, hard-packed snow was cut into blocks from 2 to 3 feet (⅔ - 1 m) long and 1 to 2 feet (⅔- ⅔ m) wide. The blocks were fitted together in a spiral that became smaller toward the top to form a dome. A hole poked through the top admitted fresh air, and seal oil lamps supplied heat. The entrance was a tunnel that trapped cold air. A thin slab of ice sometimes was set in the igloo wall for a window, and shelves for utensils were cut in the walls. The Eskimos ate and slept on a raised snow platform covered with furs.

Building Your Own Igloo

Materials Needed:

- sugar cubes, styrofoam, or packing cubes
- a piece of plywood or other flat surface
- a clear-blue piece of plastic wrap
- glue
- ruler with a strong edge

Use the sugar cubes to make the exterior of the igloo. Create this by studying the diagrams on this page. Use a ruler or similar item with an edge strong enough to shape the "ice blocks" into their finished shape. Then proceed to build your igloo on a piece of plywood or other flat surface that will support it. Use glue to hold the pieces together. Construct it so you can lift the top off it so the inside can be viewed. Use clear-blue plastic wrap for the windows.

Be creative in making or collecting the items that go inside. Make them to scale. You will need to make a few simple hunting tools, furs for the sleeping platform, and a skin to trap the cold air in the tunnel, not inside your igloo. Do not forget your seal-oil lamp for warmth and light.

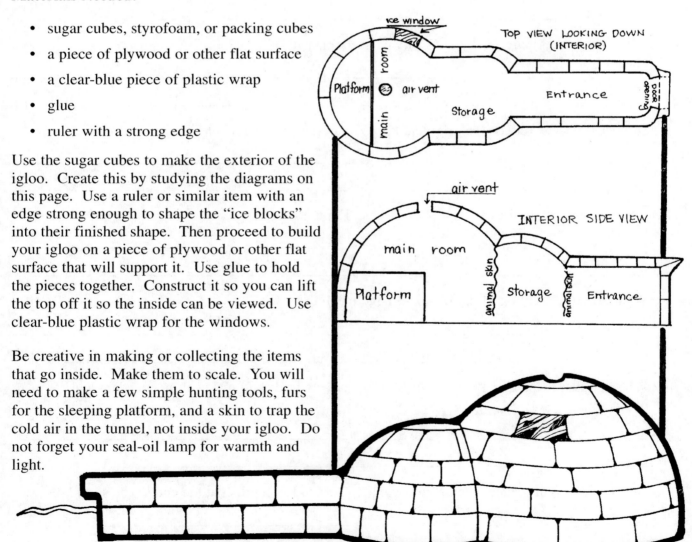

Imagine That!

This section tells how Julie is completely against the modern, civilized world. This new world seems out of harmony with the people and land of her beloved Alaska. She sees pollution, alcoholism, and airplanes that bring rich gussaks to shoot and kill animals for sport. The plane brings hunters that kill her Amaroq not for bounty, but for pleasure!

She finds out from Uma that her father is alive in a little town called Kangik. This town has a new sense of life and pride due largely to her father's influence. He starts a clothing industry and successfully raises and breeds musk-oxen. What she likes best is that it is a traditional Eskimo town that embraces all their values.

Divide into groups of four. With your group you will write an addition to *Julie of the Wolves*. Your writing will have Miyax dreaming or imagining how it will be when she arrives in Kangik. In your group answer the questions below. Use them to help in your writing.

- How does Julie imagine the town to be? What was her first impression?

  _____

  _____

- How is Julie's reunion with her father?

  _____

  _____

- What are her predictions of her future in this new setting?

  _____

  _____

- How will Julie fit into her father's life again?

  _____

  _____

Your group will also be responsible for including an illustration of the town up in the Arctic as she imagines it. Since it is a traditional Eskimo town, include a kayak and some items for hunting seal or the whale.

Astronomy: The Solar System

While alone in the wintry tundra, Miyax describes the Northern Lights. She relates how they looked like "fountains of green fire" rising from the earth. As the lights grew in intensity, it seemed that red and white lights sprayed out of the green backdrop. "The Northern Lights were dancing."

The scientific name for this phenomenon is the Aurora Borealis. They appear in the upper atmosphere at both poles. Most commonly they are viewed, as in Miyax's case, around midnight. The cause is the result of the electrical field which surrounds the earth, interacting with the solar wind. The wind excites, or ionizes, the atoms and molecules which causes the dynamic visual display.

The dancing lights are controlled by the magnetic field and the speed of the solar wind which ionizes it. The higher or more gusty the wind, the greater the ionization and visual display. The most common color is green with occasional shades of crimson and white. Auroral study is now considered a separate science. It is part of Earth science and interplanetary physics.

You will be researching some aspect of the solar system. After completing your research, you will prepare a written and visual presentation for the class. Your visual aid will be on a separate piece of paper and large enough so that everyone can see it.

Here are some sample topics:

The Solar Wind   **Asteroids**

The North Star   **Meteoroids**

The Planets   **Comets**

   • **The Inner Planets** *(Mercury, Venus, Earth, Mars)*   **The Sun**

   • **The Outer Planets** *(Jupiter, Saturn, Uranus, Neptune, Pluto)*

After the class presentations, your teacher might want to have you choose some of the most interesting ones and have the researchers go "teach" a lesson to another class in your school.

Environmental Alert

It seems that whenever Miyax gets close to "civilization," the natural beauty that she loves in her people's land is destroyed. Earlier, we see her view Barrow in a similar manner. It has houses clustered together, old boats, tires, buckets, and broken cars strewn about the town.

In this section there are old oil drums scattered throughout the landscape, and the closer she gets to Kangik the more trash Miyax sees. The author explains how in the frozen Arctic pollution is even more damaging than in other areas. "The frigid winters...prevent metals, papers, garbage and refuse from deteriorating as it does in warmer zones." So what we have here is that all these abuses to nature's purity are preserved, and the conditions can only worsen with time.

Part 1

Brainstorm with the class ways Barrow and Kangik could dispose of their trash in a more suitable manner. The purpose is to keep the countryside clean of all refuse and to prevent it from becoming an eye sore.

You and your partner are to go the Kangik town meeting prepared to make some changes. Write a speech where you address the current practice of ignoring effective supervision of refuse disposal. Your speech should consist of two parts. The first part will be on the current trend of just littering the town and the adjoining area with trash. The next part will deal with the result of your brainstorming. It will deal with solutions, listed in order, on how to combat this pollution problem. Your speech should appeal to the people's sense of community and pride in their culture.

Part 2

Working with a partner, make a poster that shows how the city of Kangik is becoming a dump. Show the types of trash that you find offensive and show how you want to get rid of them.

Part 3

With your partner, practice the speech. Decide if both or one of you will give the speech. Deliver the speech to the class.

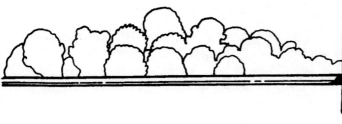

Any Questions?

When you finished reading *Julie of the Wolves*, did you have some questions that were left unanswered? Write some of your questions here.

_____

_____

_____

Work in groups or by yourself to prepare possible answers for some or all of the questions you have asked above and those written below. When you have finished your predictions, share your ideas with the class.

- What happened to Miyax before she arrived on the tundra and located Amaroq?

- How did the wolves come to accept Miyax into their den when they did not fully accept Jello?

- What was Miyax's mother like?

- Miyax learned from Martha that Kapugen left his job as manager of the reindeer herd. What was that "important" job like?

- What were the possessions that Kapugen left to go to his humble life at the seal camp?

- Why did Miyax's aunt always treat Kapugen so disrespectfully while everyone else thought he was terrific?

- Did Amy's family know that Amy had asked Miyax to come to live with them?

- What would have happened if Miyax had actually shown up at their house in San Francisco?

- With pride Kapugen reminds Miyax that she is Eskimo, a people who truly understand the earth. With this in mind, how is it they let their towns get so polluted and become victims of alcohol?

- What do you think happened after Kapugen lost Miyax to her aunt?

- When Miyax left Barrow, do you think the people stopped teasing Daniel, or would his life now be worse?

- Do you think Nusan and the townspeople looked out on the ice for Julie?

- If the land was so barren, why wouldn't an airplane spot Miyax? After all, she was on foot.

- Do you think the author was giving us a message about ourselves when she said, "There is no room in the wolf society for an animal that cannot contribute?" Explain.

- What ever happened to Kapu, Silver, and the pups?

- What was the point the author was trying to make by having Tornait die?

- Do you think it possible, knowing as you do how Kapugen felt about nature, that the pilot who flew the hunters that killed Amaroq was her father?

- Why does Miyax sing her song to Amaroq's spirit in English at the end of the story when she always sang it before in Eskimo?

Book Report Ideas

There are numerous ways to do a book report. After you have finished reading *Julie of the Wolves*, choose one method of reporting that interests you. It may be a way that your teacher suggests, an idea of your own, or one of the ways mentioned below.

- **See What I Read?**

  This report is a visual one. A model of a scene from the story can be created, or a likeness of one or more of the characters from the story can be drawn or sculpted.

- **Time Capsule**

  This report provides people living at a "future" time with the reasons *Julie of the Wolves* is such an   outstanding book and gives these "future" people reasons why it should be read. Make a time capsule design and neatly print or write your reasons inside the capsule. You may wish to bury your capsule after you have shared it with your classmates. Perhaps one day someone will find it and read *Julie of the Wolves* because of what you wrote!

- **Come To Life!**

  This report is one that lends itself to a group project. The group acts out a scene from the story and relates the significance of the scene to the entire book. Costumes and props will add to the dramatization!

- **Into The Future**

  This report predicts what might happen if *Julie of the Wolves* were to continue. It may take the form of a story in narrative, drama, or visual display.

- **A Letter to the Author**

  In the report, you can write a letter to Jean Craighead George. Tell her what you like about *Julie of the Wolves* and ask her any questions you may have about the writing of the book. You might want to give her some suggestions for a sequel! After your teacher has read it and you have made your writing the best it can be, send it to her in care of the publishing company.

- **Guess Who or What!**

  This report takes the form of several games of "Twenty Questions." The reporter gives a series of general-to-specific clues about a character from the story, and students guess the identity of the mystery character. After the character has been identified, the same reporter presents another "Twenty Questions" about an event in the story.

- **A Character Comes To Life!**

  Suppose one of the character in *Julie of the Wolves* came to life and walked into your home or classroom. This report describes what this character sees, hears, and feels as he or she experiences   the world in which you live.

- **Literary Interview**

  This report is done in pairs. One student pretends to be a character in the story. The other student will play the role of a television or radio interviewer, providing the audience with insights into the character's personality and life. It is the responsibility of the partners to create meaningful questions and appropriate responses.

Research Ideas

Describe three things you read in *Julie of the Wolves* that you want to learn more about.

_____

_____

_____

_____

As you read *Julie of the Wolves*, you encountered geographical locations, historical events, culturally diverse people, survival techniques, and a variety of animals and plants. To increase your understanding of the characters and events in the story as well as more fully recognize Jean Craighead George's craft as a writer and naturalist, research to find out more about these people, places, and things.

Work in groups to research one or more of the areas you named above or the areas that are mentioned below. Share your findings with the rest of the class in any appropriate form of oral presentation.

- State of Alaska
- Development of Alaska
- Resources of Alaska
- Brooks Range
- The North Slope
- Barrow
- Point Hope
- Fairbanks
- Gulf of Alaska
- Religion
- Symbols
- Migration across the Bering Strait
- Early Asian Hunters
- Alaskan Wildlife:
    caribou
    wolves
    whales
    foxes
    birds
    seals

- Weather Patterns
- Rivers/Mountains
- Natural Disasters
- Economy
- Eskimo Culture
    history
    ecological problems
    types of homes
    growth of towns
    clothing
    traditions
    totems
    dances
    crafts
    legends
    masks
    weapons
    family
    roles
    enemies
    food

Epilogue

Miyax returned to her father in the little Eskimo town of Kangik. Throughout the book, Miyax has been flexible and has been able to adjust and make changes to suit her circumstances. She has emerged as a young woman with a mind of her own and she has formed definite opinions on her people's culture and of the effect "civilization" has on her people. Now that she is about to begin another chapter in her life, it would be consistent to think of her new development in a positive way.

For this next activity, you are to write an epilogue of what happens after she returns to Kapugen and Ellen in her new town of Kangik.

An epilogue is an idea that originated in ancient Greek plays. After the play, one of the actors would make a speech to the audience and tell them what happened to the characters in the play after it was concluded. It was to round out the play and give it a sense of completeness.

In literature, an epilogue does much the same thing. The author writes what happened to the main characters after the main story is finished.

Epilogue Activity

You are to write an epilogue to Julie of the Wolves. You might want to include some of the following ideas:

- What happened when Miyax returned to Kangik?
- Discuss how Ellen and Miyax got along.
- How did Miyax's arrival affect her father?
- Did Miyax's father still pilot the rich "gussaks" around?
- Was there to be an Eskimo boy in her life as Miyax wanted—one that liked the old ways as she did?
- Did Miyax make any changes in the way the Eskimo people were being pushed into the "civilized" world?
- What impact did Miyax have on the village and her people?

HINT: Remember to keep the characters in the epilogue consistent with how they were throughout the story.

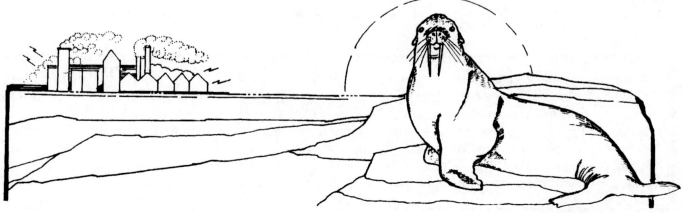

Dialogue

Dialogue is the technique used when the author has the characters talking with one another. There are certain rules that you must remember when writing in the dialogue format.

Guidelines for Writing Dialogue

1. You must use quotation marks before and after the spoken sequence and be careful to always capitalize the first letter.

    "Please write neatly."

2. A new paragraph is used after each person is finished speaking.

    "You did a fine report in science yesterday."

    "Thank you, sir."

3. When using punctuation at the end of quoted material:

    A. Periods and commas are always placed inside the closing quotes. (See example 1.)

    B. Question marks and exclamation points may be either inside or outside depending on whether the quoted material or the entire sentence is the question or the exclamation.

    The teacher asked, "Are there any questions?"

    Here the question mark is on the inside since the entire quote is the question.

    Does that student have the right "qualifications"?

    Here the entire sentence is the question, not the quote.

    Therefore, the question mark goes on the outside.

4. Use dialogue carriers to add additional meaning to the spoken words. These are not quoted.

    Miss Maple smiled warmly and said, "You are improving!"

Activity: Read the paragraph below. Take one of the ideas from it that might be confusing Julie and create a short dialogue between Julie and Ellen. Julie should express to Ellen the problem and how it confuses her. For example, why are the wolves being hunted and shot for sport? Ellen and Julie can discuss the problem and give their opinions and voice what should be done about it.

Use a separate piece of paper and include two problems to be discussed in dialogue form between Ellen and Julie. Label them as Dialogue 1 and Dialogue 2. Remember to follow the dialogue rules as stated above.

> Ellen will probably be a good influence on Julie. Julie has not really had any positive female role models in the book. Imagine that Ellen had long talks with Miyax. During these discussions, Miyax admitted her confusions such as the old ideas colliding with the new ones and the conflicts they created within her. She values that the Eskimo lives together with nature and as part of it. But the new ideas seem to say to change nature and, as we have seen, to destroy it, as in the case of pollution. She also sees how the new ideas are also corrupting the very souls of the Eskimo people as they escape to alcohol, welfare, and apathy and finally abandon their once-proud traditions.

Good-Bye, Amy

After Amaroq was gunned down from the plane by rich gussaks, Miyax cannot go to San Francisco for the "pink room is red" with Amaroq's blood. In one of Ellen's conversations, her advice for Miyax was to express her feelings on paper, to get them out of her troubled mind. Once Miyax did, she would be able to rid herself of the demons which upset her so much, and she could get on with her life. She would be able to confront life's obstacles with a clear head and solve problems more easily.

ACTIVITY 1

Pretend that you are Miyax and that you are going to write out your feelings. In this case, you will be writing about how Miyax felt about Amaroq's senseless killing. Write down Miyax's feelings and express what you think her views might be.

You should include how Miyax felt. . .

- about the wolf.

- when Amaroq was killed.

- about the hunters.

- about "civilization."

- about the practice of "hunting" animals with planes or just for "sport."

ACTIVITY 2

Write how Miyax felt about the loss of her bird. You should include the following in this activity:

- how Miyax felt about the bird while it was alive

- her feelings after it died

- any final feelings about what its death might have meant to her personally

ACTIVITY 3

For this final activity regarding Miyax's putting her troubled thoughts on paper, you are to have her write a letter to Amy. Include the following in your letter:

- that you will not be visiting her any time soon

- reasons why you will not be doing so

- relate your new life with your father who is not dead but alive and well

- describe your new stepmother and your relationship with her

- as Miyax does in the book, conclude on an upbeat note expressing hope and optimism for the future

Unit Test

Matching: Match these quotes with the characters who said them.

Martha—Daniel—Amy—Uma—Russell—Nusan—Ellen—Tornait—Miyax

1. "He, like many others, cannot tolerate alcohol."

2. "I am an Eskimo, not a gussak!"

3. "He never did anything good."

4. "Then Kapugen arrived. He was full of pride and held his head high. He soon became a leader of Kangik."

5. "When are you coming to live with us in San Francisco?"

TRUE OR FALSE: Write true or false next to each statement below.

1. Miyax is ashamed of being an Eskimo.

2. Kapugen realizes that change is inevitable.

3. The hunters in the airplane killed Kapu.

4. Martha judged Kapugen accurately when she said, "he never did anything good" after his wife died.

5. Miyax did not learn to appreciate nature during her stay on the tundra.

SHORT ANSWER: Provide a short answer for each question on the back of this paper.

1. What will probably happen to Kapu when he gets back to his family?

2. What new questions will Miyax be faced with in adjusting to Kangik?

3. Now that his daughter will be living with him again, how will Kapugen's life change?

4. After Julie buried her little Tornait, she sang a song to the spirit of Amaroq. The last line went, "That the hour of the wolf and the Eskimo is over." Describe your feelings as you read this line.

5. Discuss how Kapugen's old ways blended with the needs of civilization to save Kangik and give the Eskimo back their pride.

ESSAY: Answer these essay questions on the back of this paper.

1. Using examples from the book, discuss areas where Miyax showed growth, understanding, and appreciation of nature.

2. Miyax has no great love of civilization, as you have seen. Discuss some of the problems Miyax will have to face in her life in Kangik. Do you think she will be able to solve them and if so, how?

Response

Explain the meaning of each of these quotations from Julie of the Wolves.

Section 1:   *"Her hands trembled and her heartbeat quickened, for she was frightened, not so much of the wolves who were shy and many harpoon-shots away, but because of her desperate predicament."*

Section 1:   *"She had been watching the wolves for two days, trying to discern which of their sounds and movements expressed goodwill and friendship. Most animals had such signals."*

Section 1:   *"I am lost and the sun will not set for a month. There is no North Star to guide me."*

Section 2:   *"Open-ended tunnels reminded her of something. When the pups are about six weeks old and big enough to walk and run, the leaders move the entire group to a summer den. The cold chill of fear ran up Miyax's spine..."*

Section 2:   *"Kapugen had taught her that fear can so cripple a person that he cannot think or act. Already she was too scared to crawl."*

Section 3:   *"She stomped her foot and told him her name was Miyax."*

Section 3:   *"When one arm was pointing to the coast and the other was pointing in the direction the bird was taking, she cut off the remainder of the strip."*

Section 3:   *"The two were arguing very loudly when Martha pulled a sheet of paper from her pocket and showed it to Kapugen. No! he shouted."*

Section 3:   *"She looked at the little houses surrounded by boats, oil drums, tires, buckets, broken cars, and rags and bags, and happily followed her new parents home."*

Section 3:   *"Daniel cursed, kicked violently, and lay still. Suddenly he got to his feet and ran out of the house. 'Tomorrow, tomorrow I can, I can, can, can, ha, ha', he bleated piteously."*

Section 4:   *"Her needles and ulo, the tools of survival, were all in the pack. Shivering, she slid into bed and cried. A tear fell on the grass and froze solid."*

Section 4:   *"Miyax was worried. The oil drum she had seen when the skua flew over marked the beginning of civilization and the end of the wilderness."*

Section 4:   *"The bounty was evil to the old men at seal camp, for it encouraged killing for money, rather than need."*

Section 5:   *"She did not hear the airplane; she saw it. The low sun of noon struck its aluminum body and it sparkled like a star in the sky."*

Section 5:   *"They did not even kill him for money. She spoke of her sadness in Eskimo, for she could not recall any English."*

Section 5:   *"The pink room is red with your blood, " she said. "I cannot go there. But where can I go?"*

Section 5:   *"She pointed her boots toward Kapugen."*

Conversations

Work in size-appropriate groups to write and perform the conversations that might have occurred in each of the following situations.

- Kapugen discusses with Julie how it was that he communicated with wolves. *(2 people)*

- Kapugen, while in his seal-hunting house, tells Miyax why he left his possessions and his job after his wife died. *(2 people)*

- Miyax asks Martha what Martha meant when she said that Kapugen never "did anything good" after his wife died. *(2 people)*

- Miyax discusses why it was that Martha called her "Julie" when her real name was Miyax. *(2 people)*

- Kapugen converses with the white man after Martha told Kapugen that she was taking his daughter away from him. *(2 people)*

- Kapugen discusses with his friends, Naka and his wife, whether they would take Miyax in and let her marry their son, Daniel. *(3 people)*

- Daniel tells his folks what happened that drove his wife away. *(3 people)*

- Daniel and his family attempt to organize a search party with the military officials at Barrow. *(6 people)*

- Nusan confronts Pearl as to where Miyax ran to. *(2 people)*

- Local townspeople drink coffee and discuss Daniel and Miyax in front of a pot-bellied stove. *(3 or more people)*

- Pearl's parents ask her why she didn't check with them before giving Julie the supplies and sleeping skin and sending her to what they supposed would be her death. *(3 people)*

- Miyax, Kapugen, and Ellen talk about options for Miyax's future. *(3 people)*

- Kapugen and Ellen explain why things have to change and why Kapugen takes hunters in the plane to kill the wolves that Kapugen admittedly loves. *(2 people)*

- Kapugen tells Miyax how Miyax can fit into their lives and home if she wants to do so. *(2 people)*

- Kapugen listens to and comforts his daughter as she relates the loss of her protector and savior, Amaroq. *(2 people)*

- Kapugen, Ellen, and Miyax tell the inhabitants of Kangik that the wolf should be protected and not given up to the rich gussaks to kill for sport. *(3 people)*

- Kapugen explains his own personal plan to the town on how best to use his plane and to help protect the wolves. *(2 people)*

- Ellen tells her class of the new girl who will be joining them next week. *(7 people)*

- Ellen, Miyax, and Kapugen all discuss the reasons the town had lost its pride and spirit and the role of the Americans and the advancements they brought in this downfall. *(3 people)*

- Kapugen tells three rich gussaks that his plane is not for hire in their quest to "bag" some trophies. *(4 people)*

Bibliography of Related Reading

Nonfiction

Alexander, Bryan and Cherry Alexander. *An Eskimo Family.* Lerner, 1985.

Dunahue, Terry. *Alaska.* Watts, 1987.

Gilbreath, Alice. *The Arctic and Antarctic: Roof and Floor of the World.* Dillon, 1988.

Hirschtelder, Arlene. *Happily May I Walk: American Indians and Alaskan Natives Today.* Macmillan, 1986.

Hiscock, Bruce. *Tundra: The Arctic Land.* Macmillan, 1986.

Johnson, Sylvia. *Animals of the Polar Regions.* Lerner, 1976.

Lambert, David. *Polar Regions.* Silver, 1988.

Miller, Susanne Santoro. *Whales and Sharks and other Creatures of the Deep.* Messner, 1982.

Osinki, Alice. *The Eskimo: The Inuit and Yupic People.* Childrens, 1985.

Sandak, Cass R. *The Arctic and Antarctic.* Watts, 1988.

Smith, J.H. Greg. *Eskimos: The Inuit of the Arctic.* Rourke, 1987.

Stone, Lynn M. *The Arctic.* Childrens, 1985.

Watson, Jane Werner. *The First Americans: Tribes of North America.* Pantheon, 1980.

Yue, Charlotte, and David Yue. *The Igloo.* Houghton, 1988.

Fiction

Caswell, Helen, Ed. *Shadows from the Singing House: Eskimo Folitales.* Tuttle, 1968.

Crompton, Anne Eliot. *The Ice Trail.* Routledge, 1980.

Hewitt, Garnet. *Ytek and the Arctic Orchid: An Inuit Legend.* Vanguard, 1981.

Houston, James. *The Falcon Bow: An Arctic Legend.* Macmillan, 1986.

Houston, James. *Tilta Lictak: Eskimo Legend.* Harcourt, 1965.

Osborne, Chester G. *The Memory String.* Macmillan, 1984.

Wosmek, Frances. *A Brown Bird Singing.* Lothrop, 1986.

General Information

Bears

Barrett, Norman. *Bears.* Watts, 1988.

Graham, Ada and Frank Graham. *Bears in the Wild.* Dell, 1981.

Nentl, Jerolyn Hinshaw. *The Way of the Grizzly.* Ticknor, 1987.

Wolves

Barry, Scott. *The Kingdom of the Wolves.* Putnam, 1979.

Johnson, Sylvia A. and Alice Aamodt. *Wolf Pack: Tracking Wolves in the Wild.* Lerner, 1985.

McConoughey, Jana. *The Wolves.* Crestwood, 1983.

Sea Mammals

Crump, Donald J. Ed. *Amazing Animals of the Sea.* National Geographic, 1981.

Evans, Phyllis Roberts. *The Sea World Book of Seals and Sea Lions,* Harcourt, 1986.

Whales

Bunting, Eve. *The Sea World Book of Whales.* Harcourt, 1980.

Graham, Ada and Frank Graham. *Whale Watch.* Delacorte, 1978.

Astronomy

Branley, Franklyn M. *Sun Dogs and Shooting Stars: A Skywatcher's Calendar.* Houghton, 1980.

Jobb, Jamie. *The Night Sky Book.* Little, 1977.

Simon, Seymour. *Look to the Night Sky: An Introduction to Star Watching.* Penguin, 1979.

Answer Key

Page 10

1. Accept appropriate summaries.
2. She is looking to them as an indirect source of food.
3. She hopes to learn the way to approach the leader and thus be taken in and fed.
4. She wishes to communicate her need for assistance.
5. Kapugen is her father's name.
6. She is alone because she fled her situation in Barrow, Alaska, and is on her way to Point Hope and then to San Francisco.
7. The tundra is just a rolling plain of grass without any trees to be bent by the wind. Since there were no landmarks, she could not get a bearing on her position. Where she lived on Nunivac Island, the plants and birds pointed the way for wanderers so they could not get lost.
8. Miyax hopes to reach Point Hope where she will catch a ship.
9. At Point Hope she is going to get a job on *The North Star*. She will work her way on this ship as it takes her to San Francisco.
10. She makes a typical summer sod house like the other Eskimos would make in the tundra that season.

Page 11

1. He told her to lie down.
2. He had arched his back and narrowed his eyes drawing his ears forward. Baring his teeth, he advanced toward her.

Page 14

Explain to the students that their Reading Response Journals can be evaluated in a number of ways. Here are just a few ideas.

Personal reflections will be read by the teacher, but no corrections or letter grades will be assigned. Credit is given for effort, and all students who sincerely try will be awarded credit. If a "grade" is desired for this type of entry, you can grade according to the number of journal entries for the number of journal assignments. For example, if five journal assignments were made and the student conscientiously completes all five, then he or she should receive an "A".

Nonjudgmental teacher responses should be made as you read the journals to let the students know that you are reading and enjoying their journals. Here are some types of responses that will please your journal writers and encourage them to write more.

"You have really found what's important in the story!"

"Wow! This is interesting stuff!"

"You write so clearly, I almost feel as if I am there!"

"You seem to be able to learn from this book and apply what you learn to your life!"

"If you feel comfortable doing so, I'd like you to share your ideas with the class. They will enjoy what you've written."

If you would like to grade something for form and content, ask the students to select one of their entries and "polish it" according to the writing process.

Answer Key *(cont.)*

Page 15

1. Accept appropriate summaries.
2. They go after the weak, young, or old.
3. They pick them because they were easy kills and less dangerous.
4. She realizes that the wolves would be moving soon and getting ready for their nomadic winter life. She would not be able to keep up with them. She might die.
5. She remembers he had said, "Change your ways when fear seizes, for it usually means you are doing something wrong." She realizes that she must not depend on the wolves but on her own skills. She begins gathering her own food after this.
6. Amaroq calls her and goes to Miyax and brings her to the den. He shows the rest of the wolves that he has accepted her.
7. The fog forces a plane not to land at Barrow, and it returns to Fairbanks. That was south. She now has the north and south of her compass and can do some dead reckoning to figure out where Point Hope was, since it is west of Barrow.
8. She calls Amaroq her second father and loves him.
9. She digs through the tundra to the ice pack and has her own kind of refrigerator.
10. They give her a reason to go on living and a goal. They offer her a better life.

page 20

1. Accept appropriate answers.
2. Miyax was four years old when her mother died.
3. He changed his life and left his good job to join the Eskimo seal hunters in a small village. He was full of grief.
4. They return the bladders to the sea because the Eskimos believe that they hold the spirit of the seals in them. When they take them down to the sea, these spirits will transfer to the newborn seals and protect them.
5. At the seal camp, Kapugen tells her how wolves love you if you learn to talk to them.
6. She is upset because she values the old ways and does not want to be a gussak.
7. The winters are her special times because the gussaks are back in school, and she is alone with the real Eskimos learning the traditions and the old ways at the seal camp.
8. She will have to move away from her father and go to a gussak school.
9. She now has to do many chores for an aunt whom she does not like. She learns prejudice and gradually accepts the gussak ways of becoming ashamed of being an Eskimo. She gets a special pen pal who offers her a new life in civilized San Francisco.
10. Miyax has learned much from her father and believes that she can live off the land. In addition, she has a sleeping skin and cooking utensils to provide for her meals. She is an Eskimo, not a gussak.

page 25

1. Accept appropriate responses.
2. The wolves have already left for their nomadic winter life.
3. She tells the owl that she will see it in San Francisco.
4. Jello has raided her house, crushed it, and stolen her meat.
5. She is in very high spirits. She knows she can survive by herself.
6. The wolves kill the useless wolf, Jello.
7. She discovers that the old ways are not so bad. In fact they are very valuable and make mankind one with nature.
8. She cannot concentrate on dreams of the San Francisco life, because on the tundra everything is more beautiful than it is in San Francisco.
9. Kapu brings her a leg of caribou. Miyax is accepted and loved by the wolves now that she knows their language.
10. It reminds her that "civilization" is in conflict with nature. She loves her land, but it is always being polluted by the so called "civilized" people. She does not know at this point what she wants. She is confused.

Answer Key *(cont.)*

Page 30

A. She stood up to Jello and backed him down. Then she searched for and found her backpack with everything inside.

B. The wolves returned for her and left their scent by her. This gave her hope. She then searches and finds her pack and Jello's dead carcass.

Page 31

1. Accept appropriate responses.
2. The airplane is flying low so that rich gussaks can shoot Amaroq.
3. She thinks that because of her clothing the hunters might shoot her as well.
4. The advances brought a new, high-tech way to kill animals.
5. Miyax only speaks in Eskimo because she is an Eskimo and probably has made the decision not to become "civilized."
6. She captures his spirit on her totem.
7. They need him to lead them to capture caribou and to survive the winter.
8. It means that there are rivers, and these lead to the sea. Her journey will soon be completed.
9. Kapugen brings the old ways back to this dying town.
10. She has accepted the fact that she must fit into civilization just as her father had. It will not be easy, but her father seemed to have blended the old with the new, and she must try.

Page 42

Matching

1) Russell 2) Miyax 3) Martha 4) Uma 5) Amy

True or False

1. False
2. True
3. False
4. False
5. False

Short Answer

1. He will take over as leader of the pack.
2. How to keep her Eskimo identity. How to fit in with her father and his new life. How to accept new ideas. Accept logical answers.
3. Accept reasonable and well thought out answers.
4. Accept reasonable and well thought out answers.
5. Kapugen brought back the hunting skill to his people. He also adapted the musk-oxen to his needs and herded them. He made sweaters and scarves for the gussaks. He used the local animals for clothing and trim, and the town prospered.

Essay

1. Accept appropriate responses. Check for examples that clearly support the writer's opinion.
2. Accept fully explained responses.

Page 43

Accept all reasonable and well-supported answers.

Page 44

Perform the conversations in class. Ask students to respond to the conversations in several different ways, such as, "Are the conversations realistic?" or, "Are the words the characters say in keeping with their personalities?"